EASTER EDITION

AN INTERACTIVE AND FAMILY-FRIENDLY TRIVIA GAME OF FACT OR FICTION FOR BOYS, GIRLS, AND KIDS AGES 7-12 YEARS OLD

Copyright© 2020 by Bacchus Publishing House
ALL RIGHTS RESERVED. By purchase of this book, you have been licensed one copy for personal use only. No part of this work may be reproduced, redistributed, or used in any form or by any means without prior written permission of the publisher and copyright owner.

Don't Laugh Challenge BONUS PLAY

Join our Joke Club and get the Bonus Play PDF!

Simply send us an email to:

 **bacchuspublish@gmail.com**

and you will get the following:

- 10 BONUS hilarious jokes!
- An entry in our Monthly Giveaway of a $25 Amazon Gift card!

We draw a new winner each month and will contact you via email! Good luck!

Welcome to the ultimate lie detector game, Two Truths and a Lie - Easter Edition!

Aside from learning fun facts and testing your knowledge, this book is also a great way to spend time with friends!

How do you play?

- Grab a friend or sibling, and decide who will be 'Player 1' and 'Player 2'.

- Every round, Player 1 will start the round by reading the first set of statements to Player 2. Player 1 will then circle the answers Player 2 thinks are false. Use the guided instructions to pass the book to Player 2, and complete the rest of the round.

- Once you have both answered your questions, turn the page to check your answers and tally up your scores! The player with the least points will have to complete the End of Round DARE!

- In the event that both of you end the round with a tie, BOTH players will have to complete the dare!

- Play through all 10 Rounds and add up all your points to see who will be crowned The ULTIMATE LIE DETECTOR! In the event of a tie, continue to Round 11 - The Tie-Breaker Round where Winner Takes ALL!

- Most importantly, have fun and get ready to learn some fun facts all about Easter!

Let's get started!

PLAYER 1

Circle the false statement in each question!

Question #1

A. In Spring, you should wait to plant your flowers until the last frost.

B. Until the 14th century, Spring was called 'Lent'.

C. Easter is observed on the first Sunday after the Spring moon.

Question #2

A. Italy holds the world record for making the tallest chocolate Easter egg.

B. Approximately, 81% of people eat chocolate bunnies by starting with the ears.

C. The idea of the Easter Bunny, that we know and love, originated in Germany.

Pass the book to Player 2! ⟶

PLAYER 2

Circle the false statement in each question!

Question #3

A. When it is spring in the Northern Hemisphere, it is summer in the Southern Hemisphere.

B. The term "spring fever" is used for the feeling of restlessness and excitement caused by Spring.

C. The Disney princess, Rapunzel, has a story that features her experiencing the spring sunshine for the first time.

Question #4

A. In the original Alice in Wonderland, 'March Hare' was present at the tea party.

B. The famous Disney movie, 'Bambi', was adapted from a book written by Australian author, Felix Salten.

C. Fake chicken eggs are not becoming a problem in China.

Time to check your answers! ⟶

ANSWER KEY
Check your answers!

Question #1

Player 1 _____ /1

C. Easter is observed on the first Sunday after the spring moon.

Question #2

Player 1 _____ /1

B. Approximately, 81% of people eat chocolate bunnies by starting with the ears.

Question #3

Player 2 _____ /1

A. When it is spring in the Northern Hemisphere, it is summer in the Southern Hemisphere.

Question #4

Player 2 _____ /1

C. Fake chicken eggs are not becoming a problem in China.

Round Total

Tally up your points! Whichever player has the least amount of points has to complete the dare below. If scores result in a tie, both players must complete the dare!

 Player 1 ____ /2

 Player 2 ____ /2

DARE CHALLENGE

Stuff a handful of marshmallows in your mouth and sing 'Mary Had a Little Lamb'.

ROUND 2

PLAYER 1

Circle the false statement in each question!

Question #1

A. Old tradition says that it's good luck for families to wear new clothing on Easter.

B. In the North Pole, the beginning of spring marks six months of constant cloudy weather.

C. Families often decorate a tree with Easter eggs during the holiday to honor an old tradition.

Question #2

A. Yogi the Easter Bear, follows the story of the Easter Jamboree at Jellystone Park.

B. In Sweden, children dress up as witches and knock on neighbors' doors asking for candy, during Easter.

C. The book, 'My First Easter', follows around a baby chicken.

Pass the book to Player 2! ⟶

Circle the false statement in each question!

Question #3

A. Many songs about springtime feature elderly animals.

B. Anne Bradstreet once said, "If we had no winter, the spring would not be so pleasant."

C. While pollen is usually thought to happen in the spring, studies have shown that pollen can begin as early as January.

Question #4

A. Ancient Egyptian people exchanged gifts of eggs to symbolize new life.

B. Pretzels are associated with Easter, and are thought to have been invented by monks from Italy.

C. Honeybees are most likely to swarm in the winter in order to start new colonies.

Time to check your answers! ⟶

ANSWER KEY
Check your answers!

Question #1

Player 1 _____ /1

B. In the North Pole, the beginning of spring marks six months of constant cloudy weather.

Question #2

Player 1 _____ /1

C. The book, 'My First Easter', follows around a baby chicken.

Question #3

Player 2 _____ /1

A. Many songs about springtime feature elderly animals.

Question #4

Player 2 _____ /1

C. Honeybees are most likely to swarm in the winter in order to start new colonies.

Round Total

Tally up your points! Whichever player has the least amount of points has to complete the dare below. If scores result in a tie, both players must complete the dare!

Player 1 ____/2

Player 2 ____/2

DARE CHALLENGE

Pick something in the room and wear it on your head for the rest of the game!

ROUND 3

PLAYER 1

Circle the false statement in each question!

Question #1

A. The classic Easter movie, 'Here Comes Peter Cottontail', received a full-length sequel in 2005.

B. The third day of spring has 12 hours of daylight and 12 hours of night.

C. A famous quote by Algernon Swinburne says, "Blossom by blossom the spring begins."

Question #2

A. Approximately, 77 million cards are sent out during Easter, every year.

B. The first chocolate egg was created by Fry's of Bristol.

C. 'Hymn' is the name for a religious song of praise.

Pass the book to Player 2! ⟶

PLAYER 2

Circle the false statement in each question!

Question #3

A. Dragonflies emerge from a chrysalis in spring.

B. The 'Egg and Spoon Race' is an outdoor Easter game, that dates back to the 1800's.

C. Many families celebrate Easter by eating brunch, which is a meal eaten between breakfast and lunch time.

Question #4

A. The country of Norway celebrates Easter by reading and watching crime stories.

B. The Easter tradition of giving eggs predates the holiday.

C. A hen must be about 23-25 weeks old to lay an egg.

Time to check your answers! ⟶

ANSWER KEY
Check your answers!

Question #1

Player 1 _____ /1

B. The third day of spring has 12 hours of daylight and 12 hours of night.

Question #2

Player 1 _____ /1

A. Approximately, 77 million cards are sent out during Easter, every year.

Question #3

Player 2 _____ /1

A. Dragonflies emerge from a chrysalis in spring.

Question #4

Player 2 _____ /1

C. A hen must be about 23-25 weeks old to lay an egg.

Round Total

Tally up your points! Whichever player has the least amount of points has to complete the dare below. If scores result in a tie, both players must complete the dare!

Player 1 ____/2

Player 2 ____/2

DARE CHALLENGE

Do the worm, backwards!

PLAYER 1

Circle the false statement in each question!

Question #1

A. Also a popular children's book, 'The Hungry Caterpillar', is a common spring song for many children.

B. The period of religious fasting before Easter is known as 'Ash Wednesday'.

C. A recent study shows that 51% of adults prefer milk chocolate over dark and white chocolate.

Question #2

A. 'Here Comes the Sun' is the famous Beatles song written by George Harrison, to celebrate the return of spring to England.

B. Born in spring, baby deer are also known as 'feens'.

C. Most Easter songs share a story of religious faith.

Pass the book to Player 2! ⟶

PLAYER 2

Circle the false statement in each question!

Question #3

A. The state of Texas produces the most eggs in the United States.

B. Other than Easter, 'Groundhog Day' is an early year holiday that is also represented by an animal.

C. The 1948 musical known as 'Easter Parade' features the legendary actress, Judy Garland.

Question #4

A. Eggs contain the highest quality protein you can buy.

B. The most common activity that is celebrated for Easter tradition is the 'Egg and Spoon Race'.

C. The 'Easter Egg Roll' is a family-friendly activity, that is hosted every year on the White House's South Lawn.

Time to check your answers! ⟶

ANSWER KEY
Check your answers!

Question #1

Player 1 _____/1

B. The period of religious fasting before Easter is known as 'Ash Wednesday'.

Question #2

Player 1 _____/1

B. Born in spring, baby deer are also known as 'feens'.

Question #3

Player 2 _____/1

A. The state of Texas produces the most eggs in the United States.

Question #4

Player 2 _____/1

B. The most common activity that is celebrated for Easter tradition is the 'Egg and Spoon Race'.

Round Total

Tally up your points! Whichever player has the least amount of points has to complete the dare below. If scores result in a tie, both players must complete the dare!

 Player 1 ____/2

 Player 2 ____/2

DARE CHALLENGE

Act like a chicken and give your best "BAWK!" anytime someone laughs during the game.

ROUND 5

PLAYER 1

Circle the false statement in each question!

Question #1

A. One way that families choose to celebrate Easter is by planting flowers, in anticipation of spring.

B. A common symbol of love, 'swans' are also known as a symbol of spring.

C. E.E Cummings once said, "The earth laughs in sunshine."

Question #2

A. The age of a hen determines what color egg it will lay.

B. The springtime character, Gopher, was added to the movie, 'Winnie the Pooh and the Honey Tree', and was not in the original books.

C. Janine di Giovanni once said, "Easter is meant to be a symbol of hope, renewal, and new life."

Pass the book to Player 2! ⟶

PLAYER 2

Circle the false statement in each question!

Question #3

A. The Disney movie, 'Zootopia', features a rabbit as the main character.

B. The word 'season' comes from the Latin word 'sationem', meaning "sea tide".

C. Approximately, 57% of people plan to visit their family during the Easter holiday.

Question #4

A. Bing Crosby wrote the popular song 'Easter Parade'.

B. The wettest spring to ever occur was in 1947.

C. The meteorological spring begins on March 1st.

Time to check your answers! ⟶

ANSWER KEY
Check your answers!

Question #1

Player 1 _____ /1

C. E.E Cummings once said, "The earth laughs in sunshine."

Question #2

Player 1 _____ /1

A. The age of a hen determines what color egg it will lay.

Question #3

Player 2 _____ /1

B. The word 'season' comes from the Latin word 'sationem', meaning "sea tide".

Question #4

Player 2 _____ /1

A. Bing Crosby wrote the popular song 'Easter Parade'.

Round Total

Tally up your points! Whichever player has the least amount of points has to complete the dare below. If scores result in a tie, both players must complete the dare!

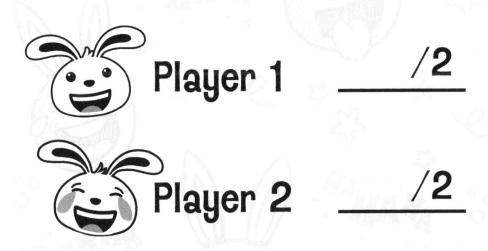

Player 1 ____/2

Player 2 ____/2

DARE CHALLENGE

Prank call your mom!

ROUND 6

PLAYER 1

Circle the false statement in each question!

Question #1

A. William Schrafft is known for inventing the jelly bean.

B. 'Very Cherry', the red colored jelly bean, is the most popular flavor of all jelly beans.

C. Migration is when animals sleep during winter and wake up in the spring.

Question #2

A. The 'Bunny Hokey Pokey' is an Easter twist on an old favorite song.

B. 'June Come She Will' is a song by Simon & Garfunkel, about the changes that spring brings.

C. Many songs that people sing around the Easter holiday talk about the idea of 'renewal'.

Pass the book to Player 2! ⟶

PLAYER 2

Circle the false statement in each question!

Question #3

A. The United States of America consumes enough jelly beans during Easter to circle the globe three times.

B. On the island of Bermuda, they release fireworks in the shape of eggs to celebrate Easter.

C. Tornadoes are a type of dangerous weather occurrence, that is most common during the springtime.

Question #4

A. The Disney film, 'A Bug's Life', was inspired by Aesop's fable, 'The Ant and the Grasshopper'.

B. The practice of painting and decorating Easter eggs using wax-resist paint comes from Ukraine.

C. In order to be less messy, most hidden Easter eggs are made out of papier-mâché.

Time to check your answers! ⟶

ANSWER KEY
Check your answers!

Question #1

Player 1 _____ /1

C. Migration is when animals sleep during winter and wake up in the spring.

Question #2

Player 1 _____ /1

B. 'June Come She Will' is a song by Simon & Garfunkel, about the changes that spring brings.

Question #3

Player 2 _____ /1

B. On the island of Bermuda, they release fireworks in the shape of eggs to celebrate Easter.

Question #4

Player 2 _____ /1

C. In order to be less messy, most hidden Easter eggs are made out of papier-mâché.

Round Total

Tally up your points! Whichever player has the least amount of points has to complete the dare below. If scores result in a tie, both players must complete the dare!

Player 1 ____/2

Player 2 ____/2

DARE CHALLENGE

Without any music, dance as crazy as you can for 30 seconds!

ROUND 7

PLAYER 1

Circle the false statement in each question!

Question #1

A. One popular Easter tradition involves using dye to color hard-boiled eggs.

B. The springtime Disney movie, 'Moana', features a sidekick named Pascal.

C. A baby rabbit is also referred to as a 'kit'.

Question #2

A. During spring, baby birds will leave the nest for the first time.

B. The tradition of the Easter Bunny arrived in the United States during the 15th century.

C. The popular candy, 'Peeps', are most commonly created in the shape of chickens.

Pass the book to Player 2! ⟶

PLAYER 2

Circle the false statement in each question!

Question #3

A. The first story of a bunny hiding eggs was published in 1680.

B. The famous proverb, "A kind word is like a spring day", came from Russia.

C. When baby hedgehogs are born in spring, they have soft hair that will turn into sharp quills within a week.

Question #4

A. The First Lady, Michelle Obama, once said "Where flowers bloom, so does hope."

B. S.D. Gordon is the author that said, "Easter spells out beauty, the rare beauty of new life."

C. In 'The Easter Egg Artists', Orson Abbott painted a bridge by himself.

Time to check your answers! ⟶

ANSWER KEY
Check your answers!

Question #1

Player 1 _____ /1

B. The springtime Disney movie, 'Moana', features a sidekick named Pascal.

Question #2

Player 1 _____ /1

B. The tradition of the Easter Bunny arrived in the United States during the 15th century.

Question #3

Player 2 _____ /1

C. When baby hedgehogs are born in spring, they have soft hair that will turn into sharp quills within a week.

Question #4

Player 2 _____ /1

A. The First Lady, Michelle Obama, once said "Where flowers bloom, so does hope."

Round Total

Tally up your points! Whichever player has the least amount of points has to complete the dare below. If scores result in a tie, both players must complete the dare!

Player 1 ____ /2

Player 2 ____ /2

DARE CHALLENGE

Sing your favorite song in the deepest voice possible.

 **PLAYER 1**

Circle the false statement in each question!

Question #1

A. During spring, the Earth's axis is tilted toward the sun.

B. The official flower of Easter is the tulip.

C. The movie, 'Rise of the Guardians', involves the Easter Bunny teaming up with Jack Frost, the Tooth Fairy, and other heroes to save the world.

Question #2

A. Irving Berlin brought the 'Easter bonnet' into American pop culture in 1933.

B. Chocolate comes from a cacao plant that grows in the ground.

C. In Lois G. Gramblin's children's novel, Peter Cottontail is out sick and replaced by a dinosaur.

Pass the book to Player 2! ⟶

PLAYER 2

Circle the false statement in each question!

Question #3

A. The famous comedian and actor, Robin Williams, once said "Spring is nature's way of saying, 'Let's party.'"

B. Rabbits are the third most popular pet in America, right behind cats and dogs.

C. One traditional Easter game, that is a local favorite in Hungary, involves rolling yarn balls down a tall hill.

Question #4

A. The name of the Winnie the Pooh Easter special is "Seasons of Giving".

B. 'Peter Rabbit' is a movie that involves four rabbits who live in Mr. McGregor's vegetable garden.

C. The Disney movie, 'Mulan', takes place during winter and ends in Spring.

Time to check your answers! ⟶

ANSWER KEY
Check your answers!

Question #1

Player 1 _____ /1

B. The official flower of Easter is the tulip.

Question #2

Player 1 _____ /1

B. Chocolate comes from a cacao plant that grows in the ground.

Question #3

Player 2 _____ /1

C. One traditional Easter game, that is a local favorite in Hungary, involves rolling yarn balls down a tall hill.

Question #4

Player 2 _____ /1

A. The name of the Winnie the Pooh Easter special is "Seasons of Giving".

Round Total

Tally up your points! Whichever player has the least amount of points has to complete the dare below. If scores result in a tie, both players must complete the dare!

Player 1 ____ /2

Player 2 ____ /2

DARE CHALLENGE

Smell one of the other player's socks for at least 20 seconds!

PLAYER 1

Circle the false statement in each question!

Question #1

A. The hair on a rabbit is also known as 'fluff'.

B. Approximately, 70% of all candy that is bought on Easter is chocolate.

C. Many families celebrate Easter by giving their children presents inside of an Easter basket.

Question #2

A. Easter is noted for having the second highest sales of candy, with Halloween sitting in first place.

B. A hen lays an average of 300 eggs every year.

C. There is a chocolate Easter bunny sculpture in Brazil that is 12 feet, 5 inches tall.

Pass the book to Player 2! ⟶

Circle the false statement in each question!

Question #3

A. The tradition of jewelled eggs comes from the country of China.

B. On Easter, girls in Hungary run down the streets as the boys throw buckets of water on them, to honor an old tradition.

C. Every year, over 17 million people will go to the doctor for allergies, which are commonly linked to spring.

Question #4

A. Springtime in the Southern Hemisphere happens between September and November.

B. The average American spends approximately $151 on Easter.

C. During Easter, more than 142 million chocolate bunnies are produced in the United States alone.

Time to check your answers! ⟶

ANSWER KEY
Check your answers!

Question #1

Player 1 _____/1

A. The hair on a rabbit is also known as 'fluff'.

Question #2

Player 1 _____/1

C. There is a chocolate Easter bunny sculpture in Brazil that is 12 feet, 5 inches tall.

Question #3

Player 2 _____/1

A. The tradition of jewelled eggs comes from the country of China.

Question #4

Player 2 _____/1

C. During Easter, more than 142 million chocolate bunnies are produced in the United States alone.

Round Total

Tally up your points! Whichever player has the least amount of points has to complete the dare below. If scores result in a tie, both players must complete the dare!

 Player 1 ____/2

 Player 2 ____/2

DARE CHALLENGE

Spin around 8-10 times, then try to walk in a straight line.

ROUND 10

PLAYER 1

Circle the false statement in each question!

Question #1

A. The first day of spring is called the 'vernal equinox'.

B. Many towns and cities across America celebrate Easter by having art festivals.

C. In 'We're Going on an Egg Hunt', by Laura Hughes, there are ten eggs to find.

Question #2

A. 'The Easter Sheep Song' is a song about one of the commonly recognized symbols of Easter.

B. In France, a giant omelette is cooked in celebration of Easter.

C. The name of Bambi's rabbit sidekick is 'Thumper'.

Pass the book to Player 2! ⟶

PLAYER 2

Circle the false statement in each question!

Question #3

A. Certain parts of the United Kingdom celebrate the beginning of Easter, by running races while tossing pancakes in the air.

B. It takes 600 cacao beans to make one pound of chocolate.

C. Migration is when animals travel from one region to another.

Question #4

A. 'Peeps', the popular Easter treat, took over an entire day to make when first introduced in 1953.

B. The movie, 'A Bunny's Life', takes a look at the beauty of spring from a new perspective.

C. Gene Autry sings the original version of 'Peter Cottontail'.

Time to check your answers! ⟶

ANSWER KEY
Check your answers!

Question #1

Player 1 _____ /1

B. Many towns and cities across America celebrate Easter by having art festivals.

Question #2

Player 1 _____ /1

A. 'The Easter Sheep Song' is a song about one of the commonly recognized symbols of Easter.

Question #3

Player 2 _____ /1

B. It takes 600 cacao beans to make one pound of chocolate.

Question #4

Player 2 _____ /1

B. The movie, 'A Bunny's Life', takes a look at the beauty of spring from a new perspective.

Round Total

Tally up your points! Whichever player has the least amount of points has to complete the dare below. If scores result in a tie, both players must complete the dare!

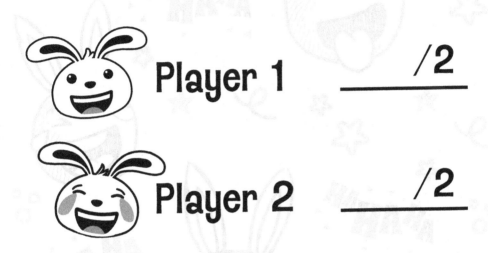

Player 1 ____/2

Player 2 ____/2

DARE CHALLENGE

Put marshmallows between your toes and leave them there for 10 minutes.

Round Total

Add up all your points from each round.
The player with the most points is crowned
THE ULTIMATE LIE DETECTOR!

In the event of a tie, continue to Round 11
for the Tie-Breaker Round!

 **Player 1** _____
Grand Total

 **Player 2** _____
Grand Total

★★★★★★★★★★★★★★★★

 The Ultimate Lie Detector

ROUND 11

Tie-Breaker Round
(Winner Takes All!)

PLAYER 1

Circle the false statement in each question!

Question #1

A. In ancient Greece, 'Persephone' was known as the 'Goddess of Spring'.

B. Only 12 out of 50 U.S. states recognize 'Good Friday' as a holiday.

C. 'The Easter Fever Is Comin' to Town' is an Easter-themed movie, whose title is a play of a popular Christmas song.

Question #2

A. Egg yolks are known to be a great source of vitamin C.

B. When the Cherry blossom begins blooming in Japan, this signals the beginning of spring.

C. The White House Easter Egg Roll tradition began in 1878.

Pass the book to Player 2! ⟶

Circle the false statement in each question!

Question #3

A. The Arctic fox changes its coat color in the Spring from white to dark brown.

B. Popular around Easter time, a 'swap race' is when an object must be passed to a team member to finish the race.

C. 'Winnie the Pooh' was inspired by a real-life forest in the United Kingdom.

Question #4

A. In the famous springtime song, Emily had a little lamb with fleece as white as snow.

B. Hot cross buns are a traditional Easter baked good, that have been the subject of many songs.

C. Easter is named after the goddess, Eostre.

Time to check your answers! ⟶

ANSWER KEY
Check your answers!

Question #1

Player 1 _____ /1

C. 'The Easter Fever Is Comin' to Town' is an Easter-themed movie, whose title is a play of a popular Christmas song.

Question #2

Player 1 _____ /1

A. Egg yolks are known to be a great source of vitamin C.

Question #3

Player 2 _____ /1

B. Popular around Easter time, a 'swap race' is when an object must be passed to a team member to finish the race.

Question #4

Player 2 _____ /1

A. In the famous springtime song, Emily had a little lamb with fleece as white as snow.

Round Total

Tally up your points! Whichever player has the most points is crowned

The Ultimate Lie Detector!

The Player with the least amount of points has to complete the final dare. If scores result in a tie, both players must complete the dare!

 Player 1 ___/2
Round Total

 Player 2 ___/2
Round Total

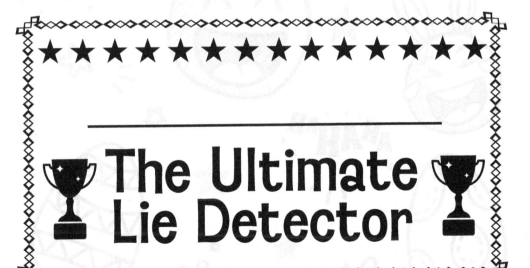

DARE CHALLENGE

Go outside and dance like a cowboy!

Check out our

Visit us at
www.DontLaughChallenge.com
to check out our newest books!

other joke books!

If you have enjoyed our book, we would love for you to review us on Amazon!

Made in the USA
Coppell, TX
25 March 2020